The Productive Developer: A Practical Handbook to Get Things Done

Table of Contents

Preface

Are you sick and tired of always feeling like you're in over your head as a developer and not getting anything done? Do you feel like you have no choice but to give up? Do you find it challenging to organize your obligations in a manner that will allow you to meet all of the deadlines that you have imposed on yourself? You may put an end to your search now that "The Productive Developer: A Practical Handbook to Getting Things Done" has arrived to save you from the muddle you've been in all this time. This book will guide you through the process of getting things done. This book will not only educate you how to complete tasks in a way that is effective but also efficient, but it will also show you how to complete tasks in such a way. This book will teach you tried-and-true methods and strategies for enhancing your productivity as a software developer, maintaining your organization, and completing the goals you have set for yourself. You may be able to put an end to procrastination for good with the assistance of "The Productive Developer," and you may also be able to look forward to a career that is both more focused and more successful.

With the assistance of this book, you will be able to achieve success in achieving both of these objectives.

About Me

Hi I am Divyansh Dwivedi. I am now working as a Team Lead (Mobile) for an MNC, and over the course of my career, I have had the opportunity to collaborate with a variety of significant corporations, like Geeks For Geeks and JP Morgan, to mention a few examples.

When I was in the sixth standard (2009), I started my road toward becoming a professional, and since then, I've worked on a variety of projects both independently and in collaboration with others. I take great delight in everything that I do as well as the long-term relationships that I've created throughout the course of my work. I have no doubt that perseverance will eventually pay off, and I am aware that each new day takes me that much closer to achieving my objectives. I have a strong interest in guiding software engineers along their professional journeys and encouraging them to realize their full potential. I have many years of experience in the industry, and I have a strong grasp of the opportunities and obstacles that are currently facing software engineers. As a result, I am here to offer you useful advice and support to help you succeed in your profession.

I am here to assist you in navigating the highs and lows that are a part of the world of software development, regardless of whether you are just beginning your career in the sector or are trying to advance to the next level. Let's put our heads together and figure out how to go where we want to go!

Chapter 1: Getting Started with Developer Productivity

How do you define developer efficiency?

Productivity in software development is measured by how quickly and easily programmers can create, test, and fix bugs in their code. It is essential to the success of any software development project as a measure of how much work can be accomplished in a given time period by a developer.

The tools and technologies employed, the developers' skill levels, and the efficiency with which projects are managed and completed are just a few of the variables that can have an effect on developer output. One crucial element of efficiency is the standard of the code being written. Code that is well-written is simpler to read, understand, and update, which reduces costs and improves productivity. Poorly written code, on the other hand, can be challenging to work with and may require substantial rework or debugging, significantly reducing productivity.

The development platform and toolset are also critical components. Coders can't do their jobs well without up-to-date programming languages, libraries, and frameworks, as well as testing and debugging software. It's important for developers to be able to focus on actually writing code rather than learning the ins and outs of the environment they're working in.

Developer efficiency relies on effective project management as well. One way to keep developers on track is to provide them with clear goals and expectations, a well-defined workflow, and all the resources they'll need. It is also crucial to have quick and simple access to all necessary documentation and resources. When trying to learn how to use a new tool or technology, or when trying to solve a problem, developers frequently need to consult documentation or other resources. In addition to boosting efficiency, having accessible and up-to-date documentation can save a lot of time and effort.

Developer efficiency also depends on the ability to work together and share information. Multiple programmers frequently team up on a single project in software development. Developers need strong communication and collaboration skills to keep their teams on the same page and moving forward. Software for managing projects, online meeting rooms, and instant messaging programmes can all help teams work together more efficiently.

The speed and simplicity with which bugs can be found and fixed in the code are also crucial considerations. Debugging is a necessary but tedious part of developing software; with the right resources at your disposal, it can be a breeze. Developers can save time and effort by having access to resources like error logs and debugging tools.

Last but not least, developers should have a pleasant and encouraging place to work. To be productive in the workplace, one must have access to all the tools they need and a positive atmosphere. The ability to work remotely or at flexible hours is one example of this, as is providing a pleasant work environment and the latest equipment.

Investing in education and training, providing access to cutting-edge tools and technologies, and establishing a streamlined process are just a few of the many ways to boost developers' output. By putting in the effort to improve these areas, businesses can better support their developers and speed up their work, which in turn speeds up the delivery of high-quality software

What it means to be a productive programmer

There are many advantages to having productive developers on staff, both for the company and the developer themselves.

The ability to finish projects more quickly and competently is a major perk of being a productive developer. Time and money are saved, and the organization is better able to meet its deadlines and provide customers with high-quality goods. Developers who are particularly efficient at their jobs are also better able to take on more responsibility, which in turn can boost their job satisfaction and open up new doors for professional growth.

Being a productive developer also means being able to write higher-quality code. Developers who are efficient at what they do are able to produce code that is clean, simple, and straightforward. Since well-written code is less likely to experience bugs or need frequent upkeep, this can be a significant time saver.

Developers who are efficient at their work often report higher levels of job satisfaction and a sense of personal achievement as a result. Developers are more likely to feel pride and accomplishment in their work when they are able to finish projects efficiently and effectively. A happier and more motivated workforce is more likely to get things done.

Being a productive developer can be advantageous for the business in addition to the individual developer. Developers who are both efficient and creative can help their companies meet the needs of their customers and succeed in their missions. Profitability, competitiveness, and overall success may improve as a result.

One advantage is that you can always learn about new tools and methods that are currently being used. The most effective developers are those who make the time to study and experiment with cutting-edge tools and methodologies that will allow them to maintain and even advance their proficiency. Because of this, the company benefits from an employee who is more productive and dedicated to their work, and the employee benefits from increased job satisfaction and the possibility of career advancement.

Being a productive developer also means you'll be able to contribute more effectively to a team setting. Developers who can effectively communicate and collaborate with their colleagues are more likely to contribute to the team's success. The result may be a happier and more productive workforce.

An added bonus of being a productive developer is the possibility of better job stability and advancement. If a company can trust its developers to complete projects on time and within budget, it is more likely to invest in their training and keep them on staff. This has the potential to improve both job stability and prospects for professional development.

Attracting and keeping top developers requires having developers who are productive. Companies that invest in their developers and give them the tools and support they require to succeed will have an easier time attracting and retaining the best programmers. The result may be more competitive businesses with better development teams.

Being a productive developer has far-reaching implications for one's professional life and the prosperity of one's company. Developers can boost their abilities, experience greater job fulfillment, and aid in the organization's success by concentrating on productivity and efficiency.

Obstacles to developer efficiency that often arise

Technical, organizational, and individual factors are just some of the many threats to developer output. Some typical difficulties include:

Poor productivity can result from developers' lack of access to the tools and resources they need to do their jobs well. The frustration and loss of productivity that can result from, say, a slow or antiquated workstation being used by a developer is just one example. Similarly, a lack of access to cutting-edge tools and libraries can cause developers to lose valuable time as they learn about and experiment with alternative solutions.

Developers may struggle to maintain focus and output if the project's goals and scope aren't clearly defined or undergo frequent iteration. For instance, a developer may have trouble making headway and may need to redo previously completed work if they are unsure of what is expected of them or if the project goals are constantly changing. Because of this, productivity may suffer as a result of misunderstandings and additional work.

Ineffective communication and teamwork: Two factors that directly affect developer output but rarely receive adequate attention. Misunderstandings, confusion, and delays can arise when developers are unable to communicate effectively with their team members or stakeholders. If a developer is working on a project and doesn't know that the project plan has been updated, they might keep working on an old version of the project, which wastes time and reduces output.

Working with a codebase that is overly complex or poorly designed can be a huge drain on a developer's time and energy, not to mention extremely frustrating. This can increase the time needed for testing and debugging, as well as the possibility of making mistakes. Delays in debugging and testing can occur, for instance, if a developer is working on a project with a codebase that is poorly organized or poorly documented.

Emails, phone calls, and other interruptions can have a devastating effect on developers' productivity. A developer, for instance, may have trouble concentrating on their work if they are frequently interrupted by emails or phone calls, and it may take them longer to get back into the flow of things after each interruption.

Burnout, a lack of motivation, and an inability to strike a good work-life balance are just a few examples of the personal factors that can have an effect on developers' output. If a programmer is experiencing burnout or stress, for instance, they may find it difficult to concentrate on their tasks at hand, resulting in lower productivity. Similarly, if a developer is having trouble juggling their work and personal commitments, they may be less than productive at work.

Time spent during the build and deployment processes can have a negative effect on developer productivity. A developer's time is valuable, and it would be better spent elsewhere if they didn't have to spend it building and deploying code to multiple environments by hand. Programmers tasked with deploying code to multiple environments or working on large, complex projects may find this especially taxing.

Productivity can be hindered if developers do not have access to adequate support and resources. This may be due to a lack of technical support, a shortage of training and development opportunities, or the absence of a mentor or other source of guidance. For instance, a developer's productivity may suffer if they have to spend a lot of time trying to figure out how to use a specific tool or technology on their own because they lack access to technical support or documentation.

A developer's productivity may suffer if they are forced to work in an environment with inefficient or ineffective development processes. For instance, a developer's time and energy could be better spent on other tasks if they weren't required to go through a time-consuming and complicated review process for every change they made. When working on complex projects with many different stakeholders, this can be especially difficult for developers.

Developers' productivity can suffer if they are not given enough freedom to make decisions and take responsibility for their work. For instance, developers' time and enthusiasm could suffer if they were required to get sign-off on every move they made. For developers accustomed to more independence, this can be especially trying, as they may feel powerless in the face of bureaucratic red tape or a lack of input into important decisions.

The productivity of developers can take a hit if they are forced to work with outdated or poorly designed development tools. For instance, a developer's productivity and efficiency can suffer if they're using a text editor that is slow or lacks necessary features.

be a pain to work with. Developers working on large or complex projects, or who rely heavily on their development tools, may find this especially difficult.

One potential cause of developers' decreased motivation and output is a lack of career advancement opportunities. A programmer, for instance, might feel less motivated and produce less work if they lacked access to training and development opportunities or knew how to advance in their career. For developers who are trying to move up in their fields but are feeling stuck or unsure of what to do next, this can be especially discouraging.

Organizations can aid developer productivity and quality by addressing these issues, which will in turn lead to the timely release of high-quality software. Investing in training and development, making sure people have easy access to the resources they need, streamlining the learning process, and providing obvious paths for advancement are all ways to achieve this goal.

Chapter 2: Developer Time Management

Developers, please take note: time management is crucial.

Developers who are able to effectively manage their time are more likely to create useful software. Having solid time management skills can aid developers in setting priorities, keeping to deadlines, and avoiding time wasters.

Good time management helps you prioritize your work, which is crucial. It's not uncommon for developers to be working on several different projects at once, and it's easy to become overwhelmed or lose focus. Developers can make the most of their time and avoid distractions by setting priorities and focusing first on the most important or time-sensitive tasks.

Better time management is another tool that can help developers finish their projects on time. Developers who are good at managing their time are more likely to finish their work on time, which can keep projects from falling behind schedule. This is of paramount significance when working under pressure to meet a strict deadline or when the stakes are extremely high.

Time management skills allow one to avoid engaging in pointless activities. It's easy for developers to lose focus and get bogged down in menial tasks that could be completed more quickly or more effectively. Developers can make the most of their time by zeroing in on the most crucial tasks and eliminating unnecessary steps.

Developers can reap additional benefits from efficient time management on top of those already mentioned.

Reducing stress and enhancing the work-life balance are two advantages. Developers are less likely to experience burnout and stress when they have a good handle on their time. The work-life balance improves and burnout is less likely to occur.

Developers can be more proactive and take charge of their work with the help of effective time management. Developers can see what must be done and how to do it if they establish goals and prioritize accordingly. Because of this, they may experience greater motivation and contentment in their work.

Effective time management can also boost teamwork and cooperation. Good time management is crucial for developers to fulfill their obligations and submit their work on schedule. As a result, their teammates can put their trust in them and work together with a greater sense of confidence.

Developers' standing and credibility in the company can benefit from better time management as well. It's easier to have faith in a developer who has a track record of reliably meeting deadlines and delivering high-quality work on time. This can improve their standing in the company and open doors to new opportunities for advancement.

Time management skills are a key factor in developers' ability to concentrate on their tasks at hand without being sidetracked. Because of this, developers may be able to complete tasks faster and more effectively, leading to increased productivity. For instance, a programmer might be more productive if they had dedicated time during which they could work without distractions.

Software developers can improve workflow efficiency and cut down on wasted time with some careful time management. Devs can get more done in less time if they prioritize the most important tasks and eliminate unnecessary steps. To illustrate, if a developer can automate or streamline their workflow, they may be able to complete tasks more quickly and make more time for other, more important tasks.

Software engineers are more likely to be able to put in the time and effort required to create high-quality products if they are efficient with their time management. This has the potential to improve outcomes and assist developers in providing higher quality output for their organization. To give one concrete example, if a developer is able to effectively manage their time and prevent feelings of overwhelm, they may be more likely to thoroughly review and test their work, which in turn results in fewer mistakes and a higher-quality final product.

Developers can use this to become more versatile and responsive in their roles. Developers who are able to effectively prioritize their work and manage their time are better able to adapt to shifting requirements and deal with obstacles. If a developer, for instance, is good at managing their workload, they might be able to shift their schedule and take on extra work when necessary without becoming stressed out.

It can aid developers in achieving a healthier work-life balance and lowering stress levels. Developers can avoid feelings of being swamped or burned out if they are skilled at prioritizing and managing their workload. By way of illustration, a developer's capacity to deal with the pressures of their job and keep a healthy work-life balance may improve if they are adept at time management and capable of carving out specific periods of time for leisure and relaxation.

Developers' standing and credibility in the company can rise as a result, opening up more promotion possibilities. Maintaining a track record of timely, high-quality output is a great way for developers to establish themselves as trustworthy and valuable members of their team, which in turn can lead to promotions. For instance, a developer's chances of being considered for promotions or other opportunities for career advancement within their organization increase if they have a track record of reliably meeting deadlines and delivering high-quality work.

It's impossible to overstate the value of efficient time management for programmers. Developers can boost productivity, reduce stress, improve the quality of their work, and advance their careers by setting priorities, sticking to deadlines, and eliminating unnecessary tasks.

Methods for productively allocating your time

It is essential for developers to be efficient and productive so that they learn to manage their time well. For programmers, some time management strategies are outlined below:

1. One of the most important aspects of time management is establishing concrete objectives and priorities. Achieving this can help you see clearly what needs to be done and prioritize accordingly. Tools like making a list of things to do and the Eisenhower matrix can help you organize your priorities and get things done in a way that makes sense.

If you have multiple tasks to complete for a project, for instance, you can make a list and arrange them in order of importance or due date. With this strategy, you can prioritize your work and complete it on time. Instead, you can use the Eisenhower matrix to rank tasks according to how critical they are and how quickly they need to be completed.

2. Make a plan and stick to it: Knowing how you'll be spending your time will allow you to more efficiently divide up your work and get it done on time. To make a schedule, divide your workday into chunks of time and

commit to completing one or more tasks during that time. Be practical about how much time you'll need to finish each task, and factor in some buffer time in case of delays.

For instance, you may organize your day by allocating time slots for distinct activities like coding, testing, and meetings. Keeping to your schedule will help you get everything done without feeling rushed or stressed.

3. Don't try to juggle too many tasks at once; contrary to popular belief, multitasking actually reduces productivity. It takes your brain some time to readjust and refocus when you switch between tasks, which can reduce your output. Avoid jumping around from one thing to another and instead focus on getting one thing done before moving on to the next.

You should, for instance, not try to code while also replying to emails; rather, finish the former before moving on to the latter. As a result, you may be able to concentrate better and get more done.

4. Taking breaks at strategic intervals has been shown to improve concentration and decrease feelings of burnout. You can use the Pomodoro technique, in which you work for a specified amount of time and then take a short break

before beginning the next work block, or you can simply schedule breaks into your day.

Every hour, for instance, you could take a short break to stretch, walk around, and breathe some fresh air. You can relax and refocus, which will increase your efficiency and decrease your stress.

5. Getting rid of interruptions will help you concentrate and make better use of your time. Turning off notifications, closing unused browser tabs, and locating a peaceful work area are all good places to start.

When you really need to concentrate on something, for instance, you can disable alerts on your phone or computer. This can help you concentrate on your work without being interrupted by constant alerts and notifications. Equally effective in reducing distractions and enhancing concentration is closing unused tabs in your web browser. Finding a peaceful place to work can help you concentrate without being interrupted by outside noise.

6. You can better manage your workload and have more time for other responsibilities if you learn to delegate some of your responsibilities to other people. Determine which of your responsibilities can be handed off to others

so that you can devote your time and energy to the ones that require your unique set of skills and knowledge.

One scenario in which delegation might be useful is when working on a project with a short deadline and a large number of individual tasks. This can help you zero in on the parts of the project that are best suited to your unique set of skills and knowledge, ultimately leading to a more successful and timely conclusion.

7. Make better use of your time by employing time-tracking tools, which will allow you to monitor your current productivity levels and determine where you can save time. If you use a time-tracking tool, you can see exactly how much time you spend on each project and where your time goes unnecessarily.

In order to monitor how much time you devote to various activities like coding, testing, and others, you can use a time-tracking tool. With this information, you can see where you're spending too much time and make changes to your process to save time.

8. Create limits: Limits can assist in time management, allowing you to fulfill all of your obligations while still having time left over. Some examples of this would be establishing regular work hours, establishing limits on

how much time you spend on various tasks, and establishing boundaries with clients or coworkers.

It's common practice, for instance, to inform one's team and clients of one's designated working hours. This can help you set reasonable goals and make sure you have time for everything you need to get done. Limiting the time you spend on things like email and meetings can help you establish boundaries with clients and coworkers.

Developers can become better at managing their time and increasing productivity by adopting these practices. Maintaining a steady routine and regularly assessing and making any necessary changes to your time management strategies are essential. Doing so will help you maximize your time and produce high-quality results in a timely manner.

9. Developers' time is easily wasted in inefficient or pointless meetings, so it's important to keep those to a minimum. In order to save time and energy, it's best to limit the number of meetings you attend and make sure that each one has a well-defined goal and agenda.

You can save time and money by using alternative methods of communication with your team, such as email or a project management tool, instead of holding weekly meetings. You can save time and energy by skipping pointless meetings and getting down to business.

10. While it's crucial to turn in high-quality work, perfectionism can be a huge time-waster. If you want to avoid perfectionism, it can help to set reasonable goals for yourself and concentrate on meeting those goals rather than striving for perfection.

For instance, rather than aiming for a perfect first draft, concentrate on producing code that satisfies the necessary specifications and can be tested and debugged. This can help you move on to the next task without getting bogged down in the weeds of the previous one.

11. Never put off doing something that needs to be done right now. Divide up the work you need to get done into smaller, more manageable chunks and give yourself a due date for each one. This can keep you from procrastinating and help you get things done before the deadline.

If you have a big project to finish, don't try to do it all at once; instead, divide it up into manageable chunks and give yourself a deadline for each one. As a result, you won't have to rush to get everything done at the last minute, and you'll have more time to focus on the project overall.

12. Recognize your time wasters The first step in breaking bad time management habits is to recognise them for what they are. To accomplish this, keep a log of your daily activities and analyze it for patterns of time loss. Knowing this can help you pinpoint inefficiencies and streamline processes.

Use a time-tracking app, for instance, to keep tabs on how long you're spending on each project. This can help you figure out what you're spending too much time on and what you can hand off to others.

Developers can increase their efficiency and productivity by following these guidelines. Consistency in your efforts to avoid time-wasting habits and a willingness to constantly evaluate and adjust your approach as necessary are both crucial. Doing so will help you get the most out of your time and finish your work promptly.

Chapter 3: Guidelines for Efficient Coding

Methods for Producing High-Quality Code

Developers must be able to write code that is both efficient and effective if they want to ship high-quality software and boost output. Methods for producing reliable and productive code are as follows:

1. Select the most effective data structures: The performance of your code can be greatly improved by selecting the most appropriate data structure for a given task. It's important to pick the right data structure for the job at hand, as different kinds of data structures perform better in certain situations.

Hash tables, for instance, are great for performing frequent searches in large datasets because they are designed specifically for that purpose. You could also use a linked list data structure, which is designed specifically for insertions and deletions, if your dataset is large and you need to modify it frequently.

2. Make your algorithms as efficient as possible. Algorithm optimization can take into account the algorithm's time complexity and space complexity.

Sorting algorithms with low time complexity include quicksort and merge sort, both of which could be useful in situations where a large amount of data needs to be sorted. Alternatively, a search algorithm with a low time complexity, such as binary search, may be preferable when working with a large dataset and performing frequent searches.

3. Take advantage of efficient code structures: the code structures you employ can also have an effect on how quickly your code executes. The number of iterations, the number of function calls, and the amount of memory used are all things that can be optimized for code performance.

If you want to reduce the runtime complexity of your code, you can use techniques like loop invariants to eliminate extra iterations. Statements that hold true before and after each iteration of a loop are called loop invariants, and they can be used to improve the efficiency of the loop by reducing the number of iterations.

Although recursive functions can be useful for finding solutions to problems, it is important to keep in mind their space complexity and limit their memory usage. While recursive functions can be more effective in some scenarios, they are not always the best solution because of their potential memory requirements and complexity.

4. Use caching to enhance your code's performance by saving frequently accessed data in memory for faster retrieval. When dealing with massive data sets or lengthy processes, this can be an invaluable tool.

Caching is used for storing data in memory that is frequently accessed, such as database query results or the results of expensive calculations. This can help you improve the efficiency of your code by reducing the number of times the same operations are executed.

5. Only perform calculations that are absolutely necessary for the task at hand to increase the efficiency of your code and avoid performing unnecessary computations.

For instance, rather than first finding the square root of a number and then squaring it, you can just square it. Having your code perform the square root calculation less frequently is a good thing.

6. You can increase your code's efficiency by using early exits, which let you leave a loop or function before all of its iterations or calls have been completed.

Example: instead of looping through a whole set of numbers to find the largest one, an early exit could be used by keeping track of the largest value along the way and breaking out of the loop as soon as a larger one is found. If your code is more efficient because of this, you can skip the extra iterations.

7. Make use of lazy evaluation to boost your code's efficiency by performing calculations only when they are actually needed.

The values of a list, for instance, can be calculated lazily, as opposed to all at once. This can make your code more efficient, especially when dealing with large datasets, by preventing extra calculations from being performed.

8. Use a technique called memoization, which caches the final results of time-consuming calculations so they can be accessed quickly in the future. Avoiding the need to recalculate the results each time they are needed can help your code run more efficiently.

To save time, you can use memoization to store the results of calculations like the Fibonacci sequence for a given number in a cache and retrieve them without redoing the work. By not having to recalculate the results, your code may run more smoothly.

9. Make use of parallelization, a technique for improving the efficiency of your code by breaking down a large task into smaller ones that can be executed in parallel.

As an illustration, parallelization can be used to split up the analysis of a large dataset into manageable chunks that can then be run in parallel. Particularly useful when processing large datasets, this can make your code run faster.

10. Instead of waiting until all of the data has been received before processing it, you can use a technique called streaming. By reducing the amount of data that must be kept in RAM, you can boost your code's performance.

In place of loading a large dataset into memory and processing it all at once, you can use streaming to process the data as it is being received, for instance. As a result, your code won't have to keep the whole dataset in memory, which is especially helpful for dealing with large datasets.

11. Use indexing, a method for quick data retrieval that involves building a data structure that connects keys with their associated values. By facilitating faster data access, this can enhance the effectiveness of your code, particularly when dealing with large datasets.

Using indexing, you can create a data structure that maps keys to values and directly access the value you're looking for, eliminating the need to iterate through the entire list of values. You can save time by not having to iterate over every item in the list, which is good for code efficiency.

12. You can speed up your data access by employing hashing, a technique that involves mapping keys to values with the help of a hash function. The speed with which you can access data, especially when dealing with large datasets, can greatly affect the efficiency of your code.

You can use hashing to map keys to values and get at the value without having to iterate through the entire list of values, for instance. As a result, your code won't have to waste time iterating over every item in the list.

13. Compress your data to make it easier to store and send across networks.

You can improve your code's efficiency, for instance, by compressing large datasets before storing them, as opposed to storing them in their raw form. When working with large datasets or sending data over a network, this can be extremely helpful.

14. Use a technique called "minification" to reduce the size of your code, making it easier to store and transmit. This is accomplished by removing white space and comments, among other things.

As an alternative to storing code in its original form, minification can be used to cut down on file size while maintaining or even increasing performance. Particularly helpful when dealing with large codebases or sending code over a network.

15. If you want to save time and effort when coding, it's a good idea to take advantage of libraries and frameworks that have already been created for similar purposes.

Use a library or framework like Hibernate or JDBC to perform database operations more efficiently, rather than writing your own database access layer. Taking advantage of this can help you save time and write more efficient code.

16. Implement design patterns. Design patterns are reusable, pre-tested solutions to common design problems that can help you save time while coding and avoid common pitfalls.

A design pattern is a reusable solution to a common design problem. For instance, the monitor pattern can be used to manage concurrent access to shared resources rather than having to write your own solution from scratch. There may be time savings and enhanced code efficiency as a result.

17. Take advantage of code reviews: this practice has other programmers look over your code and give you feedback to help you enhance its quality and performance.

As an alternative to coding in a vacuum, you can have your work reviewed by other programmers using code reviews. Finding and fixing issues like bugs and performance bottlenecks in your code can be greatly aided by this practice.

18. Use testing to ensure your code is error-free and of high quality, which will boost its dependability and performance.

Automated testing, for instance, can be used to ensure code correctness rather than relying on manual testing. By finding and fixing problems at an earlier stage, you can save time and boost your code's efficiency.

19. Put debugging to use, as it is a method for finding and fixing bugs in code that will increase its robustness and performance.

If you're having trouble with your code, you can save time and effort by using a debugger or logging to track down the source of the problem and implement a solution. Because of this, you can quickly find and fix problems in your code, which can increase its efficiency and save you time.

20. Take advantage of profiling, a method for gauging and analyzing your code's performance for the purposes of optimizing and enhancing its efficacy.

For instance, instead of supposing that your code has performance problems, you can use profiling tools like a profiler or benchmarking tool to actually measure and analyze its performance. The efficiency of your code can be increased and performance problems can be found with this method.

By using these methods, programmers are able to produce high-quality software more quickly and with less effort. Maintaining efficiency and adhering to current best practices in software development necessitates routine code reviews and enhancements. Doing so will guarantee that you ship high-quality software that serves your customers' requirements.

Advice on how to stay out of trouble and keep your code high-quality over time.

Avoiding coding errors is crucial for a developer's ability to produce high-quality software and increase efficiency. Following are some suggestions for preventing frequent errors in computer code:

1. Names for variables, functions, and other parts of your code should be as clear and descriptive as possible to help cut down on confusion and mistakes.

Using descriptive names for code elements, such as "customerName" or "totalSales," can help you understand the element's purpose and reduce the likelihood of errors.

2. Maintain a uniform style throughout your code. This includes things like indentation and formatting that are always used in the same place. This will make your code easier to read and understand, and thus less prone to mistakes.

Use a consistent indentation style, like two spaces, throughout your code rather than varying indentation styles in different sections. As a result, your code may become more comprehensible and error-free as a result.

3. Add comments to your code to help you and other programmers understand its intent and how it should work. This will help cut down on misunderstandings and mistakes.

For instance, you can add comments to your code to clarify its function and explain why it was written in a certain way rather than just leaving it as-is. You and any future developers will benefit from this in terms of comprehension and error prevention.

4. Do not release buggy software without first testing it thoroughly.

Instead of releasing buggy software before it's been tested, you could use testing methods like unit testing and integration testing to find and fix the problems that might arise. This can help your software run more smoothly and error-free.

5. Implement a version control system to keep track of your code's history and roll back to previous versions if necessary; this will help you catch mistakes before they're released and keep your users happy.

Instead of keeping track of every change you make to your code by hand, you can use a version control system like Git to keep track of everything and roll back to an earlier version if necessary. Errors are less likely, and working with other programmers is simplified, when this occurs.

6. Utilize error handling to make your code more robust against bugs and unforeseen circumstances.

Error handling methods, such as try-catch blocks, can be used to deal with and prevent errors from crashing your programme. This can help make your code more stable and less prone to bugs.

7. Implement code reviews to increase your code's quality and stability after being critiqued by other developers.

As an alternative to coding in a vacuum, you can have your work reviewed by other programmers using code reviews. The quality and dependability of your code can be enhanced by finding and fixing problems like bugs and security flaws.

8. Implement design patterns. Design patterns are reusable, pre-tested solutions to common design problems that can help you save time while coding and avoid common pitfalls.

A design pattern is a reusable solution to a common design problem. For instance, the monitor pattern can be used to manage concurrent access to shared resources rather than having to write your own solution from scratch. By avoiding these pitfalls, you can save time and increase the reliability of your code.

9. Put debugging to use, as it is a method for finding and fixing bugs in code that will increase its robustness and performance.

If you're having trouble with your code, you can save time and effort by using a debugger or logging to track down the source of the problem and implement a solution. Because of this, you can find and fix problems faster, which increases code reliability.

10. Take advantage of profiling, a method for gauging and analyzing your code's performance for the purposes of optimizing and enhancing its efficacy.

For instance, instead of supposing that your code has performance problems, you can use profiling tools like a profiler or benchmarking tool to actually measure and analyze its performance. The efficiency of your code can be increased and performance problems can be found with this method.

11. Document your code to make it more readable and understandable for yourself and other programmers.

You can document the intent and functionality of your code with techniques like comments and documentation generators, rather than just leaving it undocumented. There will be less room for error and more room for understanding, both for you and any other developers who may need to use your code.

12. Take advantage of refactoring, which entails making changes to your code's structure but not its behavior, to ensure that its quality remains consistent over time.

Refactoring techniques, such as extracting functions or renaming variables, can be used to enhance the design of your code rather than leaving it in its current state. This can help preserve the quality of your code over time and make it more readable.

13. You can keep your code's quality high over time by using linting, a process that checks your code automatically for problems like syntax errors and violations of coding style.

Use a linting tool like ESLint to automatically check your code for potential issues rather than checking it by hand. Finding and fixing bugs at an earlier stage in the development process can help you save time and keep your code high-quality over time.

14. Make use of automated testing, which entails running your code through a series of tests set up in advance and executed by a piece of software. This helps ensure that your code retains its high quality and dependability as time goes on.

You can use automated testing tools like JUnit and Selenium to test your code without having to manually test it yourself. By finding and fixing problems before they have a chance to impact the overall quality and reliability of your code, this can save you time in the long run.

15. Keep your code's quality consistent over time by implementing continuous integration, a process that automatically builds and tests your code after each change you make.

You can use a continuous integration tool like Jenkins or Travis CI to build and test your code automatically after each change, saving you time and eliminating human error. Finding and fixing bugs at an earlier stage in the development process can help you save time and keep your code high-quality over time.

16. Make use of code formatting, which entails rewriting your code so that it is automatically formatted in accordance with a particular style.

For instance, you can save time and effort by using a code formatting tool like Prettier or Clang-Format to automatically format your code so that it meets the standards of a given style. Since consistently formatted code is less likely to experience degradation over time, this can be a time-saver.

17. Maintain the quality of your code over time with static analysis, which is the process of automatically analyzing your code for potential issues like bugs and security vulnerabilities.

Use a static analysis tool like SonarQube or Coverity to automatically analyze your code for potential issues instead of doing it by hand. By doing so, time can be saved while the quality is preserved.

18. Keep your knowledge of current best practices and technologies in software development up-to-date through continuous learning to ensure that the quality of your code remains high over time.

To keep up with the latest trends in software development, for instance, you can invest in continuous learning by keeping up with the field through means such as reading articles, going to conferences, and enrolling in online courses. As a result, you can rest assured that you are employing the most up-to-date and effective methods and tools, which can help your code maintain its quality over time.

19. To save time and ensure the continued high quality of your code over time, take advantage of code libraries. These libraries contain pre-written code that can be integrated into your own projects.

Rather than writing your own code for frequently used operations like parsing a CSV file or connecting to a database, you can make use of code libraries that have already been tested and shown to work. You can save time and avoid deterioration in code quality by recycling previously tested and validated sections.

20. To save time and ensure your code's continued high quality, consider using a code generator. These tools create new lines of code based on preexisting templates or detailed specifications.

Code generators, for instance, can be used to automatically produce code based on templates or specifications rather than having to write it by hand. Because it allows you to generate code that is consistent and follows best practices, this can save you time and keep the quality of your code high over time.

21. Maintain code quality over time with continuous delivery, which entails automatically building, testing, and deploying your code after each change.

If you're tired of manually building, testing, and deploying your code after every change, consider using a continuous delivery tool like CircleCI or Azure DevOps. By keeping your code up-to-date and deployed to production, you can save time and keep it in good shape over time.

22. Using codebase analysis, which involves inspecting your code's structure and design for bugs, can help you keep your code's quality high over time.

For instance, you can use a codebase analysis tool like SonarQube or CodeScene to conduct an automated analysis of your codebase in search of problems, rather than performing the analysis by hand. Finding and fixing bugs at an earlier stage in the development process can help you save time and keep your code high-quality over time.

23. In order to keep your code's quality consistent over time, use code coverage analysis. This is the process of analyzing the amount of your code that has been put through testing.

A code coverage tool, like Istanbul or JaCoCo, can automatically analyze the proportion of your code that has been tested, so you don't have to guess. Finding and fixing untested code in this way can help you keep your code quality high over time.

24. Use dependency management to ensure your code's continued high quality as it relies on other programmes, such as libraries and frameworks.

For instance, you can use a dependency management tool like Maven or Gradle to automate the process of managing your code's dependencies rather than doing it manually. By always using the most up-to-date and stable versions of your dependencies, this can help you save time and keep your code stable over time.

25. Take advantage of security analysis, which involves checking your code for flaws in order to keep it secure over time.

If you're concerned about the safety of your code, for instance, you can use a security analysis tool like OWASP ZAP or Fortify to perform an automated scan for flaws. By finding and fixing vulnerabilities early in development, this can save time and keep your code secure over time.

26. Make use of performance analysis, which entails analyzing your code's performance to ensure that it retains its efficiency over time.

This advice will help developers avoid common coding pitfalls and provide users with high-quality software.

Chapter 4: Effective Debugging Techniques for Software Development

Methods for more productive error handling

The ability to debug code and find and fix bugs is crucial for any developer. Listed below are some best practises for bug fixing:

1. Make use of a debugger, which is a tool that lets you step through your code line by line, finding and fixing problems as you go.

You can use a debugger, either the one that comes with your development environment or a separate one, to step through your code line by line and find the source of an issue, rather than trying to find it manually.

2. Logging is the practice of recording information about programme activity in a log file or console so that problems can be located and fixed more quickly.

For instance, you can use logging to output messages to a log file or console that provide additional context on what is happening in your code, rather than trying to understand it by looking at the code itself. By giving you more insight into the workings of your code, this can speed up the process by which you locate and fix bugs.

3. Use a source code browser to quickly find and fix bugs. This tool lets you browse and search your code with minimal effort.

For instance, you can use a source code browser, either the one included with your development environment or a separate one, to quickly and easily navigate through the source code while troubleshooting.

4. Put to use a unit test framework, which is a tool for creating and running automated tests on your code in order to find and fix bugs faster.

Use a unit test framework like JUnit or NUnit to write and run automated tests for your code instead of manually testing it to find issues. Running tests automatically and spotting problems early on in the development process can save time and help you identify and fix them more efficiently.

5. Make use of a code profiler, which is a tool for measuring and analyzing your code's performance for the purpose of locating and fixing performance issues more quickly.

Use a code profiler, like the one included with your development environment or a third-party profiler, to measure and analyze your code's performance instead of doing so manually so that you can spot problems. Having access to such in-depth data on your code's performance can greatly aid in locating and fixing performance issues.

6. Use a memory profiler, which is a tool for measuring and analyzing the code's memory usage and finding and fixing memory issues more quickly.

You can use a memory profiler, such as the one included in your development environment or a third-party profiler, to measure and analyze the memory usage of your code instead of doing so manually, which can help you identify problems. By giving you specifics on how much RAM your code is actually using, this can speed up the process of finding and fixing memory-related bugs.

7. Make use of a bug tracker, which is a tool for keeping tabs on and organizing code-related problems so they can be addressed more quickly.

For instance, you can use a bug tracker like Jira or Bugzilla to keep tabs on your code's problems instead of keeping track of them by hand. By having a single location to report and organize problems, as well as the ability to prioritize them and delegate them to the most qualified team members, this can speed up the process of finding and fixing them.

These techniques will help programmers find and fix bugs in their code faster, allowing them to meet user demands with better software. If you want to find and fix bugs quickly and easily, you need to make sure your debugging process is as efficient as possible.

Methods to reduce the frequency of bug fixing

One of the primary goals of any programmer should be to reduce the amount of debugging required. How to reduce the time spent debugging:

1. To make sure your code is consistent and easy to read, use a coding style guide that specifies things like naming conventions and indentation standards.

Example: using a coding style guide to ensure your code is consistently formatted and follows best practises so that it can be read and understood by others. If your code is more comprehensible and manageable, you'll have less need for debugging.

2. Take advantage of automated testing, which involves running your code through a set of predetermined tests without your intervention.

Automated testing tools, such as JUnit and Selenium, can be used to examine your code before any problems arise, rather than relying on manual testing. By identifying and fixing problems at an early stage, this can reduce the time spent debugging.

3. Take advantage of continuous integration, which entails running automated builds and tests on your code

at regular intervals in order to spot and fix problems at an early stage in the development process.

You can use a continuous integration tool like Jenkins or Travis CI to build and test your code automatically after each change, saving you time and eliminating human error. By identifying and fixing problems at an early stage, this can reduce the time spent debugging.

4. Take advantage of pair programming, in which you and another programmer work together to write code and spot and fix bugs as they arise.

Pair programming is a method of collaborative programming in which two programmers work together to identify and resolve bugs before they have a chance to impact the project's release. By identifying and fixing problems at an early stage, this can reduce the time spent debugging.

5. Make use of code reviews: by reviewing your code with another developer, you can spot and fix problems before they have much of an impact on your project.

Code reviews are a great way for developers to work together to find and fix problems before they impact the product. By identifying and fixing problems at an early stage, this can reduce the time spent debugging.

6. Use a static code analyzer to spot problems like syntax errors and coding standards violations early on in the development process, when they are easier to fix.

You can use a static code analyzer like Checkstyle or PMD to check your code before problems arise so that you can fix them before they cause any harm. By identifying and fixing problems at an early stage, this can reduce the time spent debugging.

7. To catch and fix problems early in the development process, make use of error handling, which is the process of handling and logging errors that occur in your code.

For instance, error handling allows you to catch and record errors in your code before they can cause problems. By identifying and fixing problems at an early stage, this can reduce the time spent debugging.

8. Use defensive programming techniques such as input validation and null checking to find and fix problems before they have a chance to impact the final product.

The term "defensive programming" refers to strategies that are used to prevent errors from occurring in the first place, rather than fixing them after the fact. By identifying and fixing problems at an early stage, this can reduce the time spent debugging.

9. Take advantage of documentation, which is the process of adding documentation to your code in the form of comments or inline documentation to aid others in understanding and maintaining your code and aid in the early detection and resolution of any problems that may arise.

When writing code, documentation can be used to add comments or inline documentation that aids others in understanding and maintaining your code. If your code is more comprehensible and manageable, you'll have less need for debugging.

10. You can reduce the time spent debugging by making use of design patterns, which are reusable solutions to common software design problems that can be applied to the development of clearer, more maintainable code.

Design patterns, such as the factory pattern and the observer pattern, can be used as an alternative to writing code that is hard to understand and maintain. If your code is more comprehensible and manageable, you'll have less need for debugging.

Developers can reduce the time spent debugging and increase the quality of the software they provide to end users by adopting these practices. If you want to find bugs early in the development process and fix them, then you need to constantly evaluate and improve your development process. There will be time savings and an increase in code quality if you follow these guidelines.

Chapter 5: Methods for Effective Programming Problem Solving

Methods for efficiently addressing difficult issues

Despite the difficulty of solving complex problems, there are some approaches that can aid developers in doing so successfully:

1. Compound issues can seem insurmountable unless you take the time to break them down into more manageable chunks.

An example would be to partition a large problem into manageable chunks rather than trying to solve it all at once. As a result, you may find the problem less daunting and be able to make more rapid progress.

2. Follow a methodical process to solve the issue at hand. Complex problems are easier to handle when approached in this way.

A systematic approach, such as the scientific method or the engineering design process, can be used to solve a complex problem instead of attempting to solve it in an ad hoc manner. This can provide a more organized way to approach difficult problems.

3. Working with others to solve a problem increases your chances of success because you're able to draw on the expertise of more people.

Collaborating with others, like teammates or subject-matter experts, can help you find a better solution to a difficult problem than you would be able to find on your own, for instance. By pooling your resources, you may be able to tackle difficult problems more efficiently.

4. Making use of visual aids like diagrams and flowcharts can greatly improve your ability to comprehend and address difficult problems.

As an alternative to reading through lines of code to figure out how to fix a problem, you can use visual aids like diagrams and flowcharts to get a better grasp on the issue at hand. By doing so, you can better understand the issue at hand and start to formulate some solutions to it, which can help you tackle difficult problems more efficiently.

5. Make use of prototyping, which entails making a basic model of a solution so it can be tested and tweaked before being put into action.

You can use prototyping to create a simplified version of your solution to test and refine it before implementing it, for instance, rather than attempting to solve a complex problem all at once. Having the ability to test and refine a solution before committing to a full implementation can help you tackle complex problems more effectively.

8. Make use of heuristics, such as the 80/20 rule and the Pareto principle, to facilitate the resolution of difficult problems.

To solve a complex problem, for instance, heuristics can be used as a starting point rather than a "one size fits all" solution. By providing a structure for prioritizing and zeroing in on the most crucial aspects of the problem, this can help you tackle complex problems more efficiently.

9. Try things out and see what works; it's the best way to solve difficult problems.

Example: instead of relying on a single method to solve a complicated issue, try out a few different ones and figure out which ones work best through trial and error. If you're able to experiment and learn from your mistakes, you'll be in a much better position to take on difficult problems.

10. Make use of mental models, which are abstract simplifications of underlying concepts that can improve your ability to tackle difficult problems.

For instance, instead of blindly applying a single solution to a complex issue, you could use a mental model like "systems thinking" or "the five whys" as a starting point for your investigation. This can provide a structure for comprehending and resolving the issue at hand, making it easier to take on complex problems.

11. Make use of problem-solving frameworks, which are structured ways of approaching tough challenges head-on.

You can use problem-solving frameworks like the Six Sigma methodology or the Deming cycle to help you approach a difficult problem methodically rather than solving it on the fly. This can provide a more organized way to approach difficult problems.

12. Consider using brainstorming, which entails coming up with ideas and potential solutions to a problem in a group setting through discussion and the creation of new ideas.

A good example of this is the technique of brainstorming, which is used to come up with ideas and solutions to problems in a group setting rather than by an individual's solitary effort. As a result, you'll be able to come up with and assess a wider range of potential approaches as you work to solve difficult problems.

13. Take advantage of simulation, which involves modeling a complex system in order to test out potential solutions to an issue.

As an alternative to taking a cookie-cutter approach to solving complex problems, simulation can be used to model the system and try out various potential remedies. Effectively tackling complex problems can be facilitated by testing and evaluating potential solutions in this manner.

14. Make use of lateral thinking, also known as "creative problem solving" or "thinking outside the box," to better handle challenging situations.

To solve a difficult problem, for instance, you can use lateral thinking to generate novel and original ideas, rather than relying on tried-and-true methods. Since you'll be able to think outside the box, you'll be better able to come up with creative solutions to difficult problems.

15. You can approach difficult problems with more success if you employ design thinking, a process for

finding answers to problems by focusing on people's needs and wants.

By looking at a problem from a human-centered design perspective, for instance, design thinking can help you find a solution that will work for everyone involved. By doing so, you can better address the needs and perspectives of the people who will be implementing your solution to a complex problem.

16. In order to solve difficult problems, try using the "5 Whys" technique, which consists of repeatedly asking "why" until the underlying cause of the issue is discovered.

By asking "5 Whys," you can get to the bottom of a problem's cause and effect instead of just treating the symptoms. Effectively tackling complex problems often requires getting to the root of the issue rather than simply treating the symptoms.

17. Apply root cause analysis: This method helps you solve problems by getting to the bottom of what's causing them.

For instance, root cause analysis can be used to get to the bottom of a problem instead of just treating the symptoms. By focusing on the root cause rather than just the symptoms, this approach can help you tackle complex problems more efficiently.

18. Consider employing the Kepner-Tregoe technique, which is a method for solving problems that requires you to first recognise the issue at hand, then investigate its possible causes, then settle on the most appropriate solution, and finally put it into practise and assess its success.

The Kepner-Tregoe technique, for instance, can be used to methodically identify the problem, examine possible causes, choose the best solution, put it into action, and assess its efficacy. This can provide a more organized way to approach difficult problems.

19. Lean Six Sigma is a problem-solving approach that combines Lean principles and Six Sigma tools to boost productivity and cut down on waste, making it possible to more easily take on difficult challenges.

The Lean Six Sigma methodology, for instance, can be used to boost productivity and cut down on inefficiency instead of using a cookie-cutter approach to solve complex problems. Focusing on improving processes and getting rid of waste can make it easier to take on difficult problems.

20. Make use of the PDCA (Plan-Do-Check-Act) cycle, which is a problem-solving method that involves planning, implementing, checking, and adjusting a solution.

For instance, the PDCA cycle can be used to methodically plan, implement, check, and adjust a solution to a complex problem. Through its structured approach to problem-solving and steady iteration on the solution, this can help you tackle complex problems more efficiently.

21. The DMAIC (Define-Measure-Analyze-Improve-Control) process is a problem-solving approach that entails defining the problem, measuring the current state, analyzing the root cause, improving the process, and controlling the improvement, and can help you deal with complex problems more efficiently.

By defining the issue, measuring the current state, analyzing the root cause, enhancing the process, and controlling the improvement, the DMAIC process can be used instead of a cookie-cutter approach to solving complex problems. Having a methodical plan to follow can make it easier to solve complex problems and make incremental improvements to the solution.

22. Make use of agile methods: Scrum and Kanban are two examples of agile methodologies that use iterative and incremental approaches to solving complex problems.

For instance, instead of attempting to address a complex issue with a cookie-cutter solution, agile methodologies encourage iterative and incremental approaches. By being able to modify your strategy in response to the ever-changing nature of a problem, this can greatly improve your ability to take on difficult problems.

23. Use a fishbone diagram. This diagram is a visual tool for isolating and understanding the various causes of a problem.

For instance, the fishbone diagram can be used to deconstruct a complex problem and zero in on its underlying causes, rather than attempting a "one size fits all" solution. By providing a visual representation of the problem and facilitating the identification of the root cause, this can help you tackle complex problems more effectively.

24. Apply the SCAMPER method: This problem-solving approach involves applying a variety of creative thinking methods to a challenging problem in order to find a solution.The SCAMPER technique is a set of creative

thinking techniques that can be applied to a problem in place of a one-size-fits-all approach. These techniques include: "Substitute," "Combine," "Adapt," "Modify," "Put to other uses," "Eliminate," "Reverse," and "Scale up" or "Scale down." This will help you tackle difficult problems by stimulating original thought and exposing you to new perspectives.

25. Consider employing the Six Thinking Hats method, which suggests considering a problem from a variety of angles before deciding how best to attack it.

Instead of tackling a difficult problem head-on, the Six Thinking Hats method encourages you to consider it from a variety of angles, including the intuitive, analytical, artistic, and strategic ones. You can approach difficult problems with greater efficiency if you force yourself to think about them from various perspectives.

26. Use the A3 method: The A3 method is a structured approach to solving complex problems that entails defining the problem, identifying root causes, and implementing a solution.

For instance, the A3 problem-solving process can be used to systematically define a problem, investigate its causes, and implement an appropriate solution instead of haphazardly attempting to do so. Through its structured approach to problem-solving and steady iteration on the solution, this can help you tackle complex problems more efficiently.

These techniques allow programmers to more efficiently solve difficult issues and provide users with high-quality, functional software. If you want to be successful in dealing with difficult problems, you need to regularly assess and improve your strategy for doing so.

There will be time savings and an increase in code quality if you follow these guidelines.

Methods of dividing a difficult task into more manageable chunks

Developers who can successfully tackle complex problems by breaking them down into smaller, more manageable parts and deliver high-quality software that meets the needs of their users have an advantage over their peers. In order to tackle complex issues, developers can use the following strategies:

1. To solve a difficult problem, it can be helpful to first break it down into manageable chunks, or "divide and conquer."

Take, as an example, a programmer who is tasked with creating a social media site. The overarching objective of the project is to create a system where users can meet and exchange information. Building a user registration system, a content sharing system, and a messaging system are all manageable sub-problems that could be tackled individually by the developer in order to take on the larger problem. Developers are better able to tackle difficult problems if they first reduce them to manageable chunks that can be tackled independently.

2. With top-down decomposition, you start with the big picture in mind and work your way down to the nitty-gritty details in order to solve a difficult problem.

Think of a programmer who is tasked with creating an e-commerce website. In order to facilitate online product discovery and acquisition, the project's overarching objective is to create a platform for doing so. The developer could use top-down decomposition to partition the problem into manageable chunks before attempting to solve it. They could begin by determining the project's overarching purpose, and then break it down into more manageable chunks like creating a product catalog, shopping cart, and payment system. The developer can better understand the problem and identify its constituent parts if they begin with the end in mind and work backwards to the initial goal.

3. Bottom-up decomposition is a technique for solving complex problems by first isolating their smallest constituent parts and then reassembling them into the whole.

Take the example of a programmer who is working on a project to create a hotel booking system. The purpose of this project is to create a system through which hotel rooms can be reserved online. The developer could use bottom-up decomposition to break down the problem into manageable chunks before attempting to solve it. Identifying the smallest pieces, such as creating a form to collect user information and a database to store booking information, could help them work their way up to the larger objective. The developer can better understand the problem and identify the larger pieces that need to be solved if they start with the smallest pieces and work their way up to the ultimate goal.

4. For a more manageable solution to a difficult problem, one strategy is to perform a "functional decomposition," which involves dividing the problem into subproblems that correspond to individual functions or tasks.

Take the case of a programmer who is working on a task management app. The project's overarching objective is to develop a tool for task creation and administration. The programmer could use functional decomposition to tackle the issue by dividing it into more manageable chunks. One way they could do this is by figuring out what needs doing, or what functions, like task creation,

5. The term "use case" refers to a method of solving a difficult problem by isolating the individual steps that must be taken to reach a desired outcome.

Consider a programmer who is working on a healthcare management system. The project's overarching objective is to create software that facilitates easier patient record keeping and appointment scheduling for healthcare professionals. Use cases could help the developer tackle this difficult problem by separating it into manageable chunks. They could determine what needs to be done in order to use the system, such as creating patient files, scheduling appointments, and accessing patient files, and then construct the necessary infrastructure. The developer gains a clearer picture of the problem and its constituent parts when the actions or interactions that need to be taken are specified.

6. Make use of flowcharts, which provide a graphical representation of the procedures to be followed in order to resolve a problem. They can be useful for visualizing the steps or processes involved in a problem and thus aiding in its decomposition.

Think of a programmer who is tasked with creating a customer relationship management (CRM) system. The project's overarching objective is to construct a mechanism by which companies can administer their relationships with customers. Flowcharts would be useful for developers in this situation because they allow them to break down complex problems into manageable chunks. A flowchart could be made to illustrate the various processes that make up the CRM system, such as the building of profiles for customers, the administration of their interactions, and the examination of their data. The developer can gain a deeper understanding of the problem and its constituent parts by drawing a diagram of the process or steps involved.

7. Make use of mind maps, which are diagrams that show how various thoughts and concepts are connected to one another. They can be useful for seeing how various ideas and concepts are related to one another, which can be a significant step toward solving a more involved problem.

Take, as an example, a programmer who is tasked with creating a social media site. The overarching objective of the project is to create a system where users can meet and share information. The developer could use mind maps to partition the problem into manageable chunks before attempting to solve it. User profiles, content sharing, and community formation could all be represented graphically in a mind map. Developers gain a better grasp of the problem at hand and can zero in on the specifics that need fixing when they draw attention to the interconnections between various ideas or concepts.

8. Ask "why" several times to get to the bottom of a problem using the "5 Whys" technique. This can be a useful method for isolating the root of the problem and subsequently solving it.

For illustration's sake, picture a programmer working on a project to create an online storefront. The project's overarching objective is to construct a mechanism for commercial online product sales. The platform, however, is having difficulties with page load times. The developer could use the 5 Whys technique to tackle the problem by analyzing it from every angle. Developers can gain a better understanding of the issue at hand by tracing it back to its origins by asking the question "why" over and over again. For example: "Why is the page load time slow? Because the server is overloaded. Why is the server overloaded? Because there are too many users accessing the platform at the same time. Why are there too many users accessing the platform at the same time?"

9. The KISS (Keep It Simple, Stupid) principle is a design tenet that advocates for keeping things as straightforward as possible when trying to address complex issues. Keeping things straightforward allows you to zero in on the most crucial aspects of a problem and find a solution that works for you.

Think about a programmer who is working on a virtual reality Virtual reality (VR) game. The overarching objective is to create a game where the user is completely submerged in a computer-generated environment. However, there are bugs and stability issues plaguing the game. The developer could use the Keep It Simple, Stupid (KISS) principle to tackle the issue by first separating it into its component parts. As a result, they could concentrate on streamlining processes by cutting out as much of the

10. Make use of a simple tool like a to-do list to help you organize your work and break it down into manageable chunks. Making a list of things to do and segmenting them into manageable chunks allows you to concentrate on one thing at a time and get more done.

Take the case of a programmer who is tasked with creating a mobile application. The purpose of this project is to develop a mobile application for monitoring physical activity levels. The developer could make a list of things to do and divide the problem into smaller chunks to work on. The developer can make more rapid progress if they make a list of tasks, such as "create user profiles," "track workouts," and "analyze fitness data," and then focus on just one at a time.

11. Make use of the Pomodoro Technique, a time-management strategy based on working in 25-minute sprints followed by 5-minute breaks. Focusing on one thing at a time and taking breaks to recharge can be useful tools for tackling difficult problems in manageable chunks.

Take the example of a web designer or programmer working on a website for an organization. The purpose of this project is to create a website where people can reserve vacation homes. The programmer could use the Pomodoro Technique to tackle the problem by dividing it into smaller chunks. Employees could put in 25-minute shifts followed by 5-minute breaks. The developer will be able to focus on a single task at a time and get more done if they break up their work into shorter sessions and take frequent breaks.

12. Consider making use of the Eisenhower Matrix, a time-management device that ranks tasks according to how urgent they are and how important they are to complete. In order to make progress on difficult problems, it is helpful to organize your work in terms of importance and urgency.

Take the case of a programmer working on an application for a computer system. The project's overarching objective is the development of a programme to aid commercial enterprises in controlling their financial affairs. The Eisenhower Matrix can help the programmer tackle this difficult problem by separating it into manageable chunks. They could categorize tasks as "critical and urgent," "critical but not urgent," "not critical but urgent," or "not critical at all," allowing the developer to concentrate on the most important and urgent tasks first and get the most done.

13. The SCAMPER technique is a set of questions meant to provoke thought and inspire new ideas when faced with a challenging problem. The SCAMPER technique is a useful tool for simplifying difficult problems and coming up with new approaches to addressing them.

Think of a programmer who is tasked with creating a virtual reality game. The overarching objective is to create a game where players can explore various virtual environments. If the developer is faced with a difficult problem, like how to make the game more immersive, they can use the SCAMPER technique to break it down into manageable chunks and come up with potential solutions. Using the SCAMPER method, the developer can brainstorm possible solutions by asking themselves "substitute," "combine," "adapt," "modify," "put to other uses," "eliminate," and "reverse"-type questions.

14. Refer to the Pareto principle, also called the 80/20 rule, which states that 80% of outcomes can be attributed to just 20% of inputs. By isolating the most crucial aspects of the problem, this technique can be useful for reducing large issues to manageable chunks.

Imagine a developer working on a website for a startup company. The project's overarching objective is to create a website for the company to use for online product sales and marketing. Among the many difficult issues the developer has identified are faster page loads, a more user-friendly interface, and higher rankings in search engine results.

The developer could use the Pareto principle to zero in on the most crucial aspects of such complicated issues. Based on the data, they could prioritize fixing the top 20% of issues that are having the greatest impact on the company. The developer may, for instance, determine that page load times are the primary source of user frustration. It would make the most sense for the developer to prioritize enhancing the site's loading speed in this case, as this would have the greatest effect on the company's bottom line.

Developers can tackle the most pressing issues first by applying the Pareto principle, which involves dividing a problem into its component parts. As a result, the developer can put in more time and effort where it will have the greatest impact, speeding up the project's overall development.

Approaches to obtaining assistance in times of crisis

The ability to recognise when help is needed and to seek it out is crucial for developers who want to succeed in spite of obstacles and make meaningful progress. Here are some methods you can use to get assistance when you're stuck:

1. Locate appropriate sources: Prior to reaching out for assistance, it is crucial to locate appropriate sources that can assist with your unique issue. Forums, documentation, and in-person guides like teachers and peers are all examples of such resources. In order to get the best information possible to help you solve your problem, you need to know where to look.

If you're having trouble with a certain programming language, for instance, you could try searching for related online forums or documentation. On the other hand, if you're having trouble with a particular piece of technology, you could try searching for materials that are more narrowly focused on that piece of technology. It is possible to improve your chances of receiving a useful and correct response by locating the appropriate resources.

2. To get the help you need, you must first be able to describe your problem in detail. Some examples of this would be explaining the problem's context, outlining the steps you've taken to fix it, and describing any relevant errors or problems. The likelihood of receiving a useful and accurate response improves when the problem is clearly stated.

If you're stuck on a particular error in the code, for instance, you can detail the error message you're receiving, the code you're working with, and the steps you've taken so far to fix the issue. With this context, others will be better able to identify with your predicament and offer targeted solutions.

To get a more focused and accurate response, it's helpful to be specific and concise when asking for assistance. You can improve your chances of getting a helpful and accurate response from an online community by asking focused questions that are clear and concise.

Try new things and be receptive to criticism when asking for assistance. This may necessitate experimenting with novel equipment or techniques, or switching to a different approach to fixing the issue at hand. You can improve your chances of finding a solution to your problem by being receptive to criticism and trying out different strategies.

So, if you're stuck on a problem, you could, for instance, solicit input on how you're thinking about the issue. It's possible that other people will offer suggestions for methods or resources you can use to aid in your search for a solution. Increase your chances of solving your problem by being receptive to criticism and trying different strategies.

3. Finally, it's important to not be reluctant to seek assistance when you're struggling. Recognizing when you need help and asking for it is a sign of strength and professionalism. Seeking help is a normal and important part of the development process. It's acceptable to seek assistance, for instance, when confronted with a difficult problem that you cannot resolve on your own. It's possible that others have dealt with the same issues.

4. First, you should try to pin down where the issue originated so that you can focus your efforts and find the most useful resources. If you're having trouble with a particular programming language, for instance, it's best to find a mentor who specializes in that language rather than one who covers all of them. Finding a useful and appropriate resource is made easier if you can pin down its origin.

Recognizing your own limitations and asking for assistance when you need it are both important for making effective progress. If you're trying to solve a particularly difficult problem, but you don't have much experience in that area, it might be more productive to find someone who does. Knowing your own limitations and asking for help when you're stuck can save you time and frustration.

Before using any given resource for assistance, make sure you are familiar with its policies and guidelines by reading through its terms of service. If you're using a support forum, for instance, there may be rules about how to phrase your questions and pleas for help. You can avoid problems and make sure you're using the resource appropriately and legally if you take the time to read and comprehend the terms of service.

Seek assistance through appropriate channels, as doing so can improve the quality and timeliness of the response you receive. A project with a short deadline, for instance, may necessitate the use of a more immediate form of communication than email, such as a chat or phone call. You can improve your chances of getting a helpful and prompt response by using the right channels.

Chapter 6: Putting Developer Tasks in Order of Importance

Developer efficiency and the importance of task prioritization

Prioritizing tasks involves categorizing and ordering them according to significance and urgency. It's crucial to developers' efficiency because it helps them prioritize their work and avoid getting bogged down by less pressing or less important matters. Prioritizing tasks is crucial for developers for many reasons:

Boosts productivity: When tasks are prioritized, developers can devote their time and energy where it will have the greatest impact. If a programmer is working under pressure to meet a strict deadline, they may choose to put off answering emails or attending meetings in favor of finishing a more pressing project. Rather than getting bogged down in trivial details, this can help them focus on the most crucial aspects of the project and get it done more quickly.

Prevents burnout: Developers have a lot on their plates and can easily become overwhelmed and exhausted if they don't properly prioritize their work. A developer may experience stress and overwhelm if they have a lot of low-priority tasks piling up in their queue and they keep putting them off. Developers can avoid burnout and focus on work that matters by creating a prioritized list of tasks.

Decision-making is enhanced by the process of prioritizing tasks, as developers are forced to decide which activities are most pressing and which can wait. A developer, for instance, may have to choose between a high-priority project with an impending deadline and an urgent request for a low-priority task. In the long run, this can help them refine their ability to set priorities and make sound decisions.

Productivity rises when programmers prioritize their work in order of importance, completing more in less time. If a developer, for instance, is working toward a deadline for a particularly important project and manages to finish it early, they may find themselves with more time on their hands and be able to take on additional work. Better outcomes and a greater sense of fulfillment and satisfaction may result from this.

By setting priorities, developers can better control how they spend their time. For instance, if a programmer is working towards a deadline for a particularly important project, they may choose to devote more time to that endeavor and less to others. As a result, they will be better able to manage their time efficiently and maintain a sense of order in their lives.

The most important tasks can be completed first, reducing developer stress. If a developer, for instance, is working toward a deadline for a particularly important project and finishes it early, they may experience a sense of relief and mastery over their workload. One's general health and happiness may improve as a result.

By allowing developers to focus on the most important tasks while delegating the less important ones, prioritization of tasks can also help improve team collaboration. If a developer is working on a high-stakes project and needs to meet a strict deadline, they can free up their time and attention by handing off less crucial responsibilities to other team members.

Developers take more responsibility for their work and are better able to update stakeholders on their progress when they set priorities for their work. A developer who is working on a time-sensitive, high-priority project, for instance, may be able to provide regular updates on their progress in this way, increasing their level of openness and responsibility. A more cohesive and trustworthy group is possible as a result of this.

In conclusion, developers' productivity relies heavily on their ability to set priorities among their many duties. They are better able to make better decisions, work more efficiently, and avoid burnout as a result.

Methods for efficiently setting priorities

Developer productivity relies heavily on developers' ability to prioritize tasks, as doing so allows them to channel their efforts where they will have the greatest impact. The following are some essential factors to think about when deciding how to prioritize your work:

The first step in prioritizing your tasks is to determine what it is you're trying to accomplish and, thus, which tasks are of the utmost significance. If you're trying to get a new software product out the door, for instance, you'll want to prioritize development and testing over activities like advertising and customer service.

Once you know what you want to accomplish, you can break it down into more manageable chunks. This will help you organize your workload more efficiently. If you're working on a software development project, for instance, you can divide it up into smaller tasks like adding features or fixing bugs.

Prioritize your work after you've identified and broken it down into manageable chunks. Putting the most crucial jobs at the top of your list will help you get things done and move closer to your end goal. Critical tasks that must be completed by a certain date should be given higher priority than those that can be completed at your leisure.

Make use of productivity tools There is a wide range of productivity tools at your disposal that can assist you in setting priorities and maintaining order in your work. Software for managing projects, apps for keeping track of tasks, and apps for maintaining to-do lists are all examples of the aforementioned tools. You can use a project management tool to create a list of tasks and assign them to team members, or you can use a task tracking app to keep track of your progress and avoid falling off the rails.

Priorities should be reviewed and adjusted on a regular basis to ensure that time is being spent on the most pressing matters at hand. You'll be able to stay on course and accomplish more if you do this. If you're presented with a different set of options, for instance, you may need to reevaluate your priorities.

As a developer, it's tempting to take on everything yourself. However, when it comes to getting work done, it's often better to entrust some of the work to others. By giving other people control over less important but necessary tasks, you'll have more time to focus on the things you're good at. Reduce the likelihood of burnout and increase productivity by scaling your workload with this strategy.

Don't forget the importance of taking breaks; working continuously for long periods of time is not a prerequisite for productivity. Taking breaks gives you the opportunity to refresh and refocus, allowing you to work more efficiently when you return to your duties. Setting limits on your work time, such as not checking emails or working on weekends, can help you strike a good balance between your professional and personal life.

Feedback is a valuable tool for improving productivity, so don't be shy about asking others for their thoughts. You can learn more about your strengths and areas for improvement by soliciting feedback from your teammates, mentors, or even friends and family. Because of this, you'll be able to more easily pinpoint

Find ways to improve your productivity without resorting to previously ineffective habits or routines.

You can increase your productivity by investing in yourself and gaining new knowledge and abilities. You can improve your skills and efficiency on the job by making an effort to learn new things. This can be accomplished in a variety of ways, such as by taking a class, attending a workshop, or engaging in conversation in an online forum.

Goals that are too ambitious will only lead to frustration and disappointment. If you try to take on too much at once or set too many objectives, you may find yourself becoming overwhelmed and ineffective. Set SMART (specific, measurable, attainable, relevant, and time-bound) objectives instead (SMART). As a result, you'll be able to maintain your drive and enthusiasm and make steady progress toward your objectives.

Make use of time-saving tools and apps; these will help you get more done in less time. Tools like Trello and Asana can help you organize and prioritize your work, while JIRA can help you keep tabs on your projects and collaborate with your team. Pomodoro timers and productivity tracking apps are two more tools that can aid in maintaining focus and progress while working.

The workplace setting has a significant effect on productivity, so it's important to make adjustments as needed. Think about the environment you'll be working in and make any necessary adjustments to the lighting, temperature, and sound level. If you want to save yourself some muscle tension and weariness, ergonomic desk chairs and other office gear are a good idea.

Effectively identifying and managing distractions is essential for maintaining productivity. In order to concentrate, you should eliminate potential distractions. This could mean doing things like turning off notifications on your phone or computer, working in a quiet area, or using software like Freedom or Cold Turkey to block access to websites or applications.

Utilize automation software to free up time for more strategic pursuits by delegating menial work to a computer or a robot. This will allow you to focus on more important matters. You have access to a wide range of helpful software applications and programmes.

Through the use of automation software like Zapier or If This Then That, you can expedite your processes and free up valuable time.

Finally, if you want to increase your efficiency, try practicing mindfulness. To be mindful is to pay attention on purpose without judging what you see or how you feel in the present moment. As a result, you may be able to manage your stress and emotions more effectively, which will have a positive effect on your focus and productivity.

Overall, developers' productivity relies heavily on their ability to prioritize tasks, as doing so allows them to channel their efforts where they will have the greatest impact. Improving your ability to prioritize tasks and get more done can be accomplished by setting goals, creating actionable to-do lists, and making use of productivity tools.

Methods for avoiding the most typical problems when prioritizing work

Prioritizing tasks is essential for a developer's efficiency, but it can be difficult if not done correctly. These are some of the most common pitfalls that can be avoided with proper prioritization:

Don't prioritize based on how you feel; it's tempting to put more emphasis on things that make you happy, but doing so can cloud your judgment of what's truly important. If you're working on a software development project, for instance, and you enjoy coding a lot, you might be tempted to put that ahead of user testing and documentation. However, these ancillary activities may prove to be equally crucial to the project's completion. Task prioritization should be driven by the project's or company's impact and significance, not by individual preferences.

Don't over-prioritize: While it is necessary to assign importance to various tasks, it is also important to keep in mind that not every task should be treated as an emergency. There will be burnout and an unbalanced workload if tasks are prioritized too highly. If you're working on a project and have 10 tasks, it can be tempting to label them all as critical. However, this may cause an excessive amount of work to be done, which in turn may lead to missed deadlines or shoddy results.

An accurate assessment of each task's importance and a sensible order of priorities are both crucial.

3. Focus on high-priority tasks, but don't forget that low-priority tasks also need to be finished. If you put off dealing with them, you may end up with a mountain of work that delays the project as a whole. If you're working on a project and updating the documentation isn't a high priority, it can be easy to put it off in favor of more urgent tasks. Neglecting this duty, however, can cause additional work to pile up, which in turn can lead to missed deadlines and other problems.

Don't forget to reevaluate your priorities: Because priorities shift over time, you should regularly review your to-do list and revise it as necessary. Doing so can help you prioritize your work and get the best results. If you're working on a project and have a list of things to do, it's smart to revisit that list and adjust the priorities as necessary. It can help you prioritize what needs doing and avoid wasting time on things that are no longer high on the list.

If you are having trouble setting priorities or are feeling overwhelmed, don't hesitate to ask for assistance. If you're part of a team, this can be especially helpful because different people on the team may see things differently and have suggestions for how you can better prioritize your work. If you're working on a project and can't figure out which steps to take first, for instance, it might be a good idea to talk to your coworkers or superior about it.

Do not forget to establish due dates; doing so will help guarantee that your work will be completed in a timely fashion.

Mistakenly placing less importance on long-term objectives: It's simple to get bogged down in the here-and-now, but it's crucial to keep the big picture in mind when deciding how to allocate your time. Developers often have to choose between fixing bugs in the current release and adding new features for future versions of their software. However, the new function may better serve the company's long-term interests and, as such, warrants higher priority.

Lacking an accurate estimation of the amount of time required to complete a task. Because they had an inaccurate estimation of how much time it would take, a programmer, for example, might choose to postpone other tasks in order to focus on reworking a significant portion of code instead. It's possible that there will be problems with timeliness and a buildup of work.

Neglecting to take into account that certain tasks may be reliant on the completion of others. Developers, for instance, may need to wrap up activity A before moving on to activity B. Delays in completing Task B and the entire project may result from not giving Task A sufficient priority.

It's crucial to differentiate between urgent and important tasks, otherwise you risk letting the former take precedence over the latter. A developer may put off adding a new feature that would enhance the user experience in favor of fixing a bug that is causing the software to crash, for instance. Even though the bug fix is essential, the new feature may prove to be more valuable in the long run.

Not realizing when you have too much on your plate and failing to consider delegating some of your responsibilities to other team members. When developers get too busy, they may forget to hand off some work to their less experienced colleagues. The result may be a sluggish workflow and a pileup of unfinished work.

A developer who takes on tasks in the order in which they are assigned, without giving any thought to the importance or urgency of each task, is failing to prioritize. This can cause one to neglect more important tasks in favor of those that seem less urgent. A developer may, for instance, spend hours on a minor bug in a low-priority feature while ignoring a major issue caused by a high-priority bug.

Failure to take into account the big picture: When setting priorities, it's crucial to keep the project's or company's long-term goals in mind. For instance, a programmer may choose to work on a new feature for the product instead of fixing a critical bug because the new feature is more interesting or exciting. But if you're having serious problems because of the bug, Fixing the bug is more crucial for the product's long-term success than gaining users at this time.

Overestimating the time you have available to complete tasks can lead to taking on too much, which can lead to stress and burnout. A developer, for instance, may fail to account for the time necessary to complete a complex task and may take on too much work at once, which can lead to missed deadlines and decreased productivity.

The failure to regularly reevaluate priorities can lead to unsatisfactory outcomes because priorities must be readjusted as new information becomes available. It's not uncommon for a developer's initial priorities for a project to shift as the work unfolds. Priorities should be reviewed on a regular basis to make sure that time is being spent on the most crucial activities.

Failing to delegate means you have too much on your plate and aren't using your team or outside resources to their full potential. A developer who is already overworked may make matters worse by taking on even more responsibilities, which can lead to stress and a drop in output. The developer can stay healthy and focused on the most important tasks by delegating some of their work or recruiting outside help.

Developers can boost their productivity and contribute more to the success of their projects and organizations if they avoid these pitfalls and carefully prioritize their tasks.

Chapter 8: Staying focused as a programmer

Distractions and their effects on programmers' efficiency

As they can cause problems with workflow and concentration, distractions can have a major effect on developers' output. These are some common sources of distraction for programmers:

The constant pinging of your inbox or your chat app can be very distracting, especially if you're tempted to stop what you're doing to check your inbox or respond to a message.

The constant stream of updates and notifications on social media sites can be extremely distracting.

Distracting noises, like those made by talking coworkers or blaring music, can make it tough to get work done.

Even though they're often necessary, meetings can be a serious disruption to your day because they take you away from your tasks for a while and make it hard to get back into a groove when you're done.

A person's productivity can be negatively impacted if they are constantly diverted from their work by personal errands like checking their bank statements or scheduling doctor's appointments.

Every day, as developers, we have to fight off the temptations of other things that could be more important. Notifications, emails, meetings, or even the natural inclination to put off doing work are all examples of the kinds of things that can serve as distractions. Although it's inevitable that we'll face distractions at some point, if we don't learn to control them, they can seriously hamper our work.

Some considerations regarding the influence of interruptions on programmers' efficiency are as follows:

Getting back into the swing of things after being sidetracked by something like a phone call or a notification can be a major pain. It can be challenging to get back into a task after being distracted, for example if a developer is working on a complex problem and receives a notification on their phone.

Distractions can make it harder to maintain focus on a task for an extended period of time. It can be challenging to stay focused on a single task when you're constantly being distracted by things like notifications and interruptions from coworkers, as a developer might experience while working on a project.

Ultimately, distractions can have a negative effect on productivity by reducing how much work is accomplished in a given time frame. It may take a developer longer to finish a task if they are frequently interrupted while working on it.

As a result of making it more challenging to meet deadlines and finish tasks on time, distractions can add to an already stressful situation. The developer may feel stressed and overwhelmed, for instance, if they are working on a task with a short deadline but are constantly interrupted.

Distractions can be a hindrance to productivity because they make it harder to focus on what needs to be done. When working on a task that requires intense concentration, a developer who is easily sidetracked may find it difficult to make any headway.

Time lost to interruptions is time not spent productively on tasks at hand. There may be a significant amount of time lost as you try to get back into the flow of things.

If you are easily sidetracked, it will be more difficult to complete your work in a timely manner and meet your deadlines. You and your team could suffer as a result of this.

Stress and exhaustion can result from being constantly interrupted while working, preventing you from completing any one task for any length of time. The effects on your efficiency and health may not be immediately noticeable, but they may emerge over time.

Tools like task blockers and noise-canceling headphones can help developers stay focused and get more done. They can also schedule time to check email and social media and cut down on unnecessary meetings. It's also important to be self-aware and try to pinpoint any habitual sources of distraction, like checking your phone too often, that you can work on reducing. Developers can boost their productivity and get more done in less time by eliminating unnecessary interruptions.

Methods to keep from getting sidetracked and techniques for staying concentrated in the workplace

Developers care deeply about productivity because it has a direct bearing on their capacity to meet deadlines without sacrificing quality. Distractions are a major cause of lost productivity. Notifications, emails, phone calls, social media, and other forms of electronic communication are just some examples of common sources of distraction. These interruptions can cause a developer to lose concentration and stop working efficiently. Some techniques to help you concentrate:

Identifying what causes you distraction is the first step toward eliminating those sources. Various sources of distraction exist, including but not limited to: electronic alerts, visitors to your workstation, and ambient noise. Once you've identified your sources of distraction, you can begin to take steps toward reducing or eliminating them altogether.

Do not be distracted by your phone or computer's notifications if you need to focus on an important task. To prevent this, only check your notifications at predetermined times during the day, or disable notifications for apps that aren't absolutely necessary. In this way, you can keep your mind on your work rather than being distracted by notifications.

Dedicate a certain amount of time each day to work; doing so will help you focus and get more done if you have a clear break between your work and personal life. It could be as easy as setting aside a specific time each day to get work done, or finding a quiet place to work where you can concentrate.

To focus in a loud or chaotic environment, noise-canceling headphones are an absolute must. To lessen the annoyance, put in some earplugs or put on some headphones that have noise cancellation capabilities. Use the deep focus / concentration music playlist instead of your usual music if you need to concentrate. More than anything else, it will make it difficult for you to concentrate.

Make use of a productivity app or tool: These days, there is no shortage of digital resources that can assist you in maintaining your concentration and warding off distractions. Distraction-blocking features, such as those found in website aggregators, time tracking apps, and task management suites, are just some of the ways that these programmes can assist you in maintaining focus and getting things done.

If you're having trouble focusing because of interruptions from coworkers, it may help to let them know what you're going through. Explain that you're currently working on something and would appreciate it if they could return later or contact you via email or chat instead.

Taking frequent breaks can help you maintain focus and put off interruptions for longer than you might think. Taking brief breaks to move around, stretch, and refocus on your work can be extremely beneficial. If you don't want to waste too much time because of being sidetracked, it's a good idea to limit your breaks to a specific amount of time.

You can use a tool to prevent yourself from accessing potentially disruptive websites, such as social media or news websites. Using these aids can help you keep your mind on the task at hand and resist the urge to check your phone or computer.

Having clear boundaries with your coworkers can help you focus on your work and avoid unnecessary interruptions if you perform your duties in an office setting. For example, you could schedule meetings and conversations during specific times of the day or shut the door to your office when you need to concentrate.

The Pomodoro Technique is a time-management strategy in which you work in 25-minute sessions followed by 5-minute breaks. When you schedule your work and breaks at predetermined times, it's easier to stay on task and less likely to be distracted.

Disable alerts on your phone and computer; they can be a major distraction. One strategy for reducing interruptions while working involves limiting the frequency with which you are alerted to new messages or turning off notifications altogether.

The ability to focus and avoid interruptions is greatly enhanced by establishing regular work and break times. This can include doing things like checking emails and messages at set times during the day and taking breaks at consistent times throughout the workday.

Make use of a to-do list, which can serve as a useful guide for the day's activities, allowing you to concentrate on getting things done and warding off distractions. As a result, you'll be less likely to waste time on unimportant details or divert your attention elsewhere.

Making sure you have a place to work without any potential sources of distraction is the last piece of the puzzle. Some examples of this would be working in a different location or at a different time of day, or clearing the clutter from your desk. If you set up your space so that it encourages concentration and productivity, you'll be in a much better position to block out interruptions.

Utilize aids that enable heightened levels of concentration. There are a variety of programmes and software packages designed to improve your ability to pay attention to tasks at hand. Tools like Forest and the Pomodoro Technique are great for keeping you on track when it comes to your work, while apps like Freedom can block distracting websites and apps.

To maintain focus and enthusiasm on the job, it is helpful to establish specific goals. If you want to make progress and stay on track, one strategy is to divide your goals into smaller, more manageable tasks.

You can keep your attention and save time by keeping your belongings in order. As an illustration, you can use apps like Trello and Asana to manage your projects and stay on top of your to-do list.

Keep your mind from wandering by practicing mindfulness, which involves bringing your attention back to the present moment rather than letting it wander off to other things. Meditation or simply taking some deep breaths could be helpful here.

Because lack of sleep is associated with a decrease in focus and an increase in susceptibility to distractions, getting a good night's sleep is an effective strategy for maintaining focus and boosting productivity.

Chapter 9: The Mindset of an Effective Programmer

Developer efficiency and frame of mind

Developers' mindsets have been shown to have a substantial impact on their work habits, resilience in the face of adversity, and overall output. A negative mindset can lead to procrastination, a lack of motivation, and eventually giving up, while a positive mindset can keep developers motivated, focused, and productive.

Positive thinkers in the IT field are more likely to tackle problems head-on and come up with innovative solutions, making them better equipped to take on new challenges. They have more of a tendency to keep going when things get tough, regardless of the obstacles they encounter. In contrast, developers with a pessimistic outlook may be less likely to take a proactive approach to their work and more likely to give up when they encounter obstacles.

The way in which developers talk to themselves is another important aspect of mindset in developer productivity. Developers can keep their motivation up and their minds on the task at hand by engaging in positive self-talk rather than negative self-criticism. Moreover, developers can keep a positive outlook and stay motivated by practicing gratitude and concentrating on the things that are going well rather than dwelling on negative thoughts or setbacks.

Those programmers who have a "growth mindset," the conviction that their skills can be honed and honed further over time, may be more eager to take on difficult tasks. On the other hand, developers who hold the "fixed mindset" (the conviction that their abilities are fixed and cannot be changed) may be less motivated and may stunt their development.

The developer's mindset is very important for their productivity because it can affect how they approach their work and deal with difficulties. In contrast, a negative mindset can cause developers to procrastinate, lose focus, and become reactive rather than proactive when faced with problems.

Having the "growth mindset," the conviction that one's talents and skills can be honed and enhanced with effort and practice, can be especially helpful for programmers. Developers who adopt this frame of mind are more likely to be self-motivated and open to taking on new challenges, which in turn helps them maintain their productivity and advance in their careers.

Maintaining a positive and productive frame of mind is essential for developers, and developers can do so by practicing gratitude, talking positively to themselves, and keeping an optimistic outlook. Despite obstacles, these methods can help developers maintain their drive and concentration.

The developer's state of mind has a profound effect on their output. Keeping a constructive outlook can aid developers in maintaining energy and focus, solving issues with initiative and originality, and adjusting to new requirements. On the other hand, if you have a pessimistic outlook, you might find yourself putting things off, lacking motivation, avoiding challenges, and ultimately giving up.

Overall, a developer's frame of mind plays a significant role in their productivity, as it can have a profound effect on how they approach and perform their work. Developers can be more effective and productive in their work if they adopt a constructive and successful frame of mind that helps them maintain motivation, focus, and initiative.

Methods for fostering a positive frame of mind

An individual programmer's frame of mind has a major impact on how much they get done. A negative outlook, on the other hand, can decrease motivation and divert attention, leading to decreased productivity and eventual burnout. Some examples of how a developer's frame of mind can affect their output:

Devs can keep their motivation up and their focus sharp by setting goals that are both challenging and attainable. To stay on track with a software development project, for instance, a developer might divide the task of implementing a particular feature into smaller, more manageable chunks with their own deadlines. Keeping a positive frame of mind can help developers avoid procrastination and keep them focused on their work.

Perseverance: Having a mindset of perseverance can help developers maintain their motivation and focus despite obstacles or setbacks. When a developer is trying to solve a difficult problem and hits a snag, having a persistent mindset can help them keep plugging away at it. Having a positive outlook can give developers the mental fortitude they need to finish challenging work when they might otherwise give up or feel overwhelmed by it.

One who has a growth mindset sees potential in themselves and believes they can strengthen it through deliberate practice and reflection. This has the potential to increase motivation and openness to new experiences and opportunities. To illustrate, a developer with a growth mindset might be more open to learning new languages and technologies in order to expand their toolkit. In contrast, a fixed mindset, the conviction that one's talents are innate and unchangeable, can stifle productivity and stunt development.

Developers who keep a positive frame of mind are more likely to tackle problems with initiative and originality, while those with a pessimistic outlook are more likely to avoid the issue altogether or fail to muster the motivation to find a solution. A developer with a positive outlook, for instance, may be more motivated to learn more about the problem at hand and to work with others to find a workable solution.

Developers can avoid procrastination and feelings of being overwhelmed by keeping a positive frame of mind and focusing on the most important tasks at hand. A developer with a positive frame of mind, for instance, may be more likely to make a daily or weekly schedule to keep track of their work and ensure that their most pressing responsibilities get completed first. On the other hand, if you're in a bad mood, you might put off doing the work that needs to be done because you feel like you can't possibly get it all done.

Ability to recover quickly from setbacks and keep working on a problem is a trait fostered by cultivating resilience. Instead of giving up or feeling defeated, a negative mindset can help developers adapt to changing circumstances and stay motivated. A developer with a resilient mindset, for instance, would be more likely to draw wisdom from setbacks and try again with a revised strategy.

Developers can keep a positive outlook and keep their motivation high by practicing gratitude. Developers are more likely to maintain focus and output if they pay attention to the positives rather than ruminating on the negatives. By way of illustration, rather than giving up when confronted with a challenge,

Present moment awareness (or "mindfulness") can aid programmers in maintaining concentration and warding off distractions. Developers can be more efficient and avoid distractions if they focus on the work at hand.

Skills in time management: Being able to prioritize work, establish due dates, and manage one's time efficiently are all important aspects of time management that can help developers maintain focus and get more done.

Developers can maintain their productivity through the use of established habits and routines, which provide them with a sense of structure and make it simpler to concentrate on their work. Setting up a work environment that encourages concentration and productivity may involve blocking off specific times for work, scheduling regular breaks, and eliminating distractions.

Developers can better focus and stay free of interruptions if they establish limits on when and where they can get work done. Limiting the number of times per day you check your email or social media, or limiting the number of projects you work on at once, are all good examples.

To avoid becoming overwhelmed and losing focus, developers should seek support when they need it. This may entail asking a coworker for advice or consulting a superior for direction.

Self-criticism is counterproductive and often leads to feelings of failure and exhaustion, so it's important to show yourself some compassion when you fall short. Successful people consistently practice self-compassion and accept that making mistakes is an integral part of learning.

Mistakes are an inevitable part of the educational process, so instead of berating yourself for them, you could try reframing the situation. This can help you keep a positive outlook and work on getting better instead of beating yourself up over the error.

A lack of breaks can lead to burnout and a decrease in productivity, so it's important to take them. Maintaining concentration and output may require periodic breaks in which the worker can relax and rejuvenate.

Take breaks every hour or so to refresh yourself, instead of working nonstop for eight hours. Taking a break like this can help you keep your concentration and keep you working efficiently.

Take care of your stress levels; if they're too high, it could affect your productivity and lead to burnout. Meditation, exercise, and therapy are all effective ways to deal with stress that can help you keep a positive outlook and get more done.

To prevent stress from building up, you could, for instance, practice relaxation methods like meditation or physical activity. You may find that this aids your concentration and productivity.

In conclusion, a developer's motivation, focus, and output can all benefit from adopting a more optimistic outlook. But a pessimistic outlook can dampen productivity and cause burnout. Developers need a positive frame of mind if they are going to meet their objectives and operate at peak efficiency.

Chapter 10: Wrap-Up

Next steps for increasing your developer productivity

Increasing developer output is an ongoing task that necessitates the use of a well-rounded set of techniques, programmes, and mental approaches. The following are some recommendations for how to proceed in order to maximize your efficiency:

Take some time to think about your current workflow and see where you might be losing time or productivity. Is there work that takes more time than it needs to? Are you employing the most efficient methods possible? If you can pinpoint these problems, you can improve your processes and work more efficiently.

Try out a variety of methods; improving developer output cannot be solved with a single method. The things that help one person may not help another. You need to try out various approaches and resources to determine what works best for you.

Focus and determination can be maintained if one sets goals that are both challenging and attainable. Create objectives that are SMART (specific, measurable, attainable, relevant, and time-bound) (SMART).

Organize your work in order of importance to help you stay focused and get things done faster. Focus and get more done with time management tools like the Eisenhower matrix and the Pomodoro technique.

Break up your work with regular breaks; this will help you maintain energy and focus. Every hour or so, take a short break to walk around, stretch, and unwind.

You must learn to manage your time well if you want to boost developer output. Keep on top of your workload by using calendars, to-do lists, and time management programmes.

Develop an optimistic perspective. Your output will benefit greatly from your increased optimism. Do things like exercising, meditating, and keeping a journal to boost your mood and sense of well-being.

You can boost developer output and advance your career by adopting these practices. In order to maintain productivity and reach your objectives, it is essential to regularly evaluate your processes and make adjustments.